MOVING UP WITH SCIENCE

THE BODY

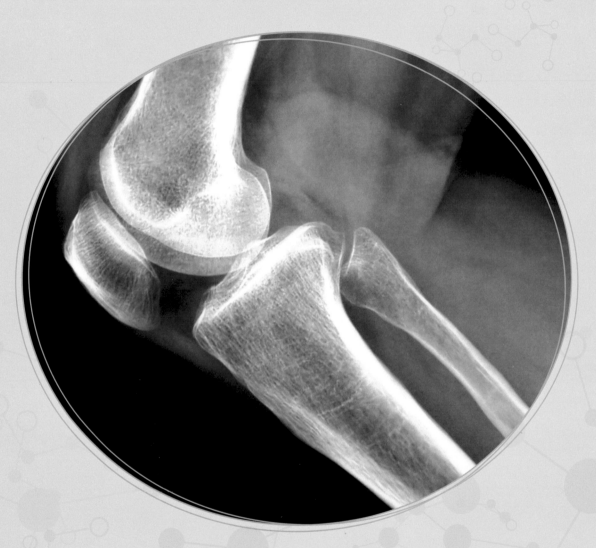

Peter Riley

W

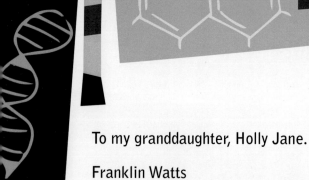

To my granddaughter, Holly Jane.

Franklin Watts
Published in Great Britain in 2016 by The Watts Publishing Group
Text copyright © Peter Riley 2015

Editor: Hayley Fairhead
Designer: Elaine Wilkinson

ISBN: 978 1 4451 3540 3
Dewey classification number: 610

Printed in China

Franklin Watts
An imprint of Hachette Children's Group
Part of The Watts Publishing Group
Carmelite House, 50 Victoria Embankment, London EC4Y 0DZ

An Hachette UK Company
www.hachette.co.uk
www.franklinwatts.co.uk

MIX
Paper from responsible sources
FSC
www.fsc.org
FSC® C104740

Photo acknowledgments: Africa Studio/Shutterstock: 21cr. Alila Medical Media/Shutterstock: 15. antpkr/Shutterstock: 10c. Berc/istock: front cover c. Blue Ring Media/Shutterstock: 19br. Maxim Chumash/Shutterstock: 25c. Matthew Cole/Shutterstock: 6. eAlisa/Shutterstock: 21b. Vasilev Evgenii/Shutterstock: 11b, 28. Miroslav Hiavko/Shutterstock: 11t. Hurst Photo/Shutterstock: 20c. ifong/Shutterstock: 22b. Ramona Kaulitzki/Shutterstock: 8t. Sebastian Kaulitzki/Shutterstock: 19tl. Matt Knoth/Shutterstock: 26br. D Kucharski K Kucharska/Shutterstock: 13b. Robyn Mackenzie/Shutterstock: 21cl. marinerock/Shutterstock: 24b. Monkey Business Images/Shutterstock: 22t. Pakhnyushchy/Shutterstock: 12bl. Ake Sak/Shutterstock: 5b. Sanyanwuji/Shutterstock: 1, 7. Peter Schwarz/Shutterstock: 25t. Sciencepics/Shutterstock: 5c, 18. S-F/Shutterstock: 21t, 31t. smileimage9/Shutterstock: 4. Andrey Smirnov/Shutterstock: 23t. Yakin Sonat/Shutterstock: 23c. Anna Subbotina/Shutterstock: 13c. svtrotof/Shutterstock: 24t. 3drenderings/Shutterstock: 13t. Visivastudio/Shutterstock: 12tr. Valentyn Volker/Shutterstock: 20b. Shane White/Shutterstock: 14b. wonderwall/Shutterstock: 26bl.

Artwork: John Alston pages 26–27.
All other photographs by Leon Hargreaves.
With thanks to our models Sebastian Smith-Beatty and Layomi Obanubi.

Contents

Words in **bold** can be found in the glossary on pages 28–29.

Animal bodies

Animal bodies come in all sorts of different shapes and sizes. Some bodies have two legs or four, six, eight, thirty or more and some have no legs at all. Bodies can be covered with hair, feathers, scales, tough armour or skin. Humans are animals with two legs and a body covered with skin.

Signs of life

All bodies carry out seven activities of life. The first six are breathing, feeding, moving, using your **senses** to find out about your surroundings, getting rid of waste and growing. The seventh takes place when an animal is fully grown. This is reproduction or breeding – making new animals.

Animal bodies have different coverings. The large body of a rhinoceros is covered in tough skin. The smaller body of a bird is covered in feathers.

Body parts

A body has many parts. The human body is divided into a head, **torso** and limbs (arms and legs). Most body parts are hidden from view. They are inside the body, under the skin. Each body part or organ carries out different activities that help to keep the body alive. For example, the heart pumps blood around the body and the lungs control breathing. In this book we shall be looking at the parts of the body that help us move and the parts that help us eat and digest our food.

chest

abdomen

The torso is the largest part of the body. It is divided into the chest and the abdomen.

The first scientists found out what was inside the body by cutting open bodies of dead animals, such as frogs and mice.

Today, scientists can use **X-ray** machines and **MRI scanners** to see inside living bodies. This MRI scan shows the brain inside the human head.

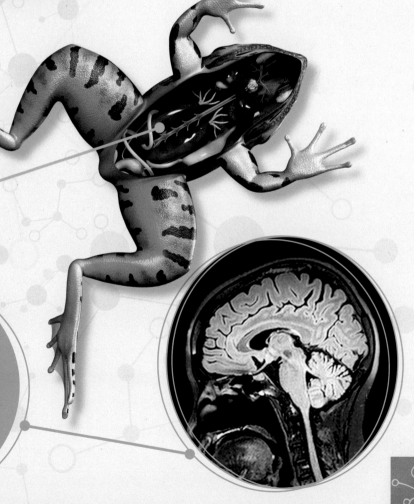

The human skeleton

Many animals have skeletons, including humans. The human skeleton is inside the body. It performs three tasks. It gives us support, it protects parts of our body and it helps us to move.

Support

The skeleton is made of strong, hard bones. They fit together to hold us up. If you did not have a skeleton you would be very floppy!

The largest bone in the human skeleton is in the leg above the knee. The smallest bones are found deep inside the ears.

Protection

The bones of the skull form a hard case to protect your **brain**. The bones of your ribs make a cage, which protects your heart and lungs. The backbone protects the **spinal cord**, which is made of **nerves** that connect your brain to the rest of your body.

skull

lower jaw

rib

humerus

radius

backbone

ulna

pelvis

femur

patella

tibia

fibula

Movement

The place where two bones meet is called a joint. Bones can move inside the joints. The end of each bone is covered in slippery **cartilage** to help the bones move more easily. Bones are connected to joints with tough, non-stretchy **ligaments**, which hold them firmly in place.

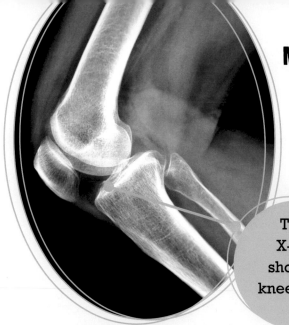

This X-ray shows a knee joint.

Paper bones

Scientists sometimes make models to use in experiments. Find out if thicker bones are stronger than thinner bones by making model bones out of rolled-up newspaper.

Equipment:

- rolls of newspaper in a variety of thicknesses
- kitchen weights

1.
Hold a thin paper roll between your hands or rest it between the back of two chairs. Put a weight on the paper roll and put a box underneath to catch it if it falls. Add more weights until the roll bends.

2.
Repeat the experiment with a thicker paper roll. The thicker the roll, the more weight it can carry before it bends. The thicker your bones, the stronger they are. Your leg bones are thick, this makes them strong enough to support your whole body.

Muscles

There are over 640 muscles in your body. Muscles make a body move.

How muscles work
Muscles are attached to the skeleton. When a muscle **contracts** it can make a bone, or bones, move. If a muscle contracts, it gets shorter and feels harder.

This artwork shows the main muscles of the human body. Each muscle moves a part of the body. Certain parts of the body, such as the arm, need several muscles to help them move.

You can feel your muscles move if you frown, then stick your fingers in your cheeks and smile. When you smile the muscles in your cheeks contract. Seventeen muscles are used to make you smile.

Tendons

Muscles are attached to bones by **tendons**. You can feel them in the inside of your elbow joint when you bend your arm. You can also feel them at the back of the knee when you sit down.

Working together

Once a muscle has become short and hard, it needs help to relax and lengthen. Muscles are arranged so that when one muscle moves and gets shorter, another muscle stretches, ready to pull it back. You can investigate how two muscles in your arm work together.

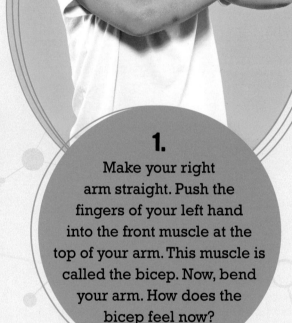

1.
Make your right arm straight. Push the fingers of your left hand into the front muscle at the top of your arm. This muscle is called the bicep. Now, bend your arm. How does the bicep feel now?

2.
Now keep your arm bent and push the fingers of your left hand into the back muscle at the top of your arm. This is called the tricep muscle. Straighten your arm again. How does your tricep feel as you move your arm back?

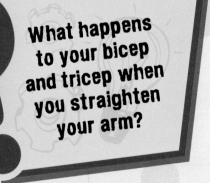

? What happens to your bicep and tricep when you straighten your arm?

Animal skeletons

Animals can be divided up into two groups according to the type of skeleton they have. Animals which have a skeleton made of bone and cartilage are called vertebrates. Animals that do not have this type of skeleton are called invertebrates.

A fish is a vertebrate because it has a bony backbone.

Vertebrates

Vertebrates have a large number of bones, all linked together by joints, which form the animal's backbone or spine. Each bone is called a **vertebra**, and lots of vertebra are called vertebrae. There are five groups of vertebrates: fish, **amphibians**, **reptiles**, birds and **mammals**.

You can feel the vertebrae in your backbone if you rub your fingers down the middle of your back. Each lump you feel is the top of a vertebra.

Invertebrates

The largest group of invertebrates is made up of animals that have a hard, protective case around their body called an **exoskeleton**. These animals are called arthropods. They are divided into four sub-groups: insects; centipedes and millipedes; spiders and scorpions; and crustaceans.

A stag beetle is an insect. Its exoskeleton acts like a suit of armour to keep it safe from rivals when it fights.

If you watch a snail moving, you can see its muscles rippling as it uses the water inside it for support.

Water bodies

Some invertebrates do not have any hard parts to support them. They have water sealed into their bodies instead, which gives them support. These invertebrates include jellyfish, worms and molluscs, such as snails and slugs.

Try this activity to get an idea of how strong a slug's water-sealed body is. Pour water into a balloon, hold the end shut and rest it on a table. Add a weight on top of the balloon. What happens?

Movement in animals

As in humans, muscles and skeletons work together to make animals move. Each animal uses its skeleton and muscles in different ways.

Muscles pull a fish's body into a curved shape, which pushes on the water and moves the fish forwards.

Movement in fish

The vertebrae of a fish are fixed together with lots of joints so that the backbone is flexible and can bend when the muscles on either side pull on it. This helps a fish move through the water.

Movement in reptiles and amphibians

Newts, salamanders, lizards and crocodiles have four legs and a flexible backbone. Their muscles work with their skeletons to make their bodies into a 'S' shape, which throws their legs forwards so they can walk and run.

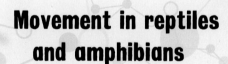

A lizard moves by throwing both legs on one side forward at the same time.

Movement in birds

The backbone of a bird is rigid and fixed tightly to its ribs. This makes the skeleton firm enough to support the bird's flight muscles. When the flight muscles shorten and lengthen, the wings flap up and down and push on the air, which makes the bird rise up. When the wings are tipped backwards and flapped, the bird moves forwards.

A bird's breastbone is very large. It has many flight muscles attached to it.

Movement in insects

The middle part of an insect's body is called the **thorax**. In flying insects, the thorax is packed with muscles that move the wings.

When the muscles inside the thorax move, the dragonfly's wings move up and down.

Each segment of an earthworm's body stretches and shrinks to help it move.

Movement in worms

Worms have water sealed into their body, which is divided into sections called **segments**. The muscles in each segment help the worm move along. Tiny hairs on its skin help it to grip the soil as it moves.

Teeth

Teeth are used to cut, rip and grind food until it is small enough to swallow. Humans cut and rip food with their sharp front teeth. The tongue passes the food to big, blunt back teeth for grinding, before the food is swallowed.

Teeth come in different shapes and sizes according to the job they do.

Milk teeth

Humans have two sets of teeth during their lifetime: milk teeth and adult teeth. Milk teeth begin to grow through when a human is around six months old and are a complete set of 20 teeth by around three years old. At around six years old, the milk teeth start to fall out and a second set begins to grow in their place. This adult set of 32 teeth should last for the rest of a human's life.

Your milk teeth fall out to make way for your adult teeth.

Adult teeth

There are four types of adult teeth. These are the incisors, canines, premolars and molars.

Incisors

The incisor teeth have wide, sharp tops like the blade of a knife. We use them to bite into our food.

Canines

The canine teeth are pointed and can look a bit like fangs. We use them to tear up tough food like meat.

Premolars and molars

The sharp premolars and molars have lumps called cusps, which help to grind up all types of food.

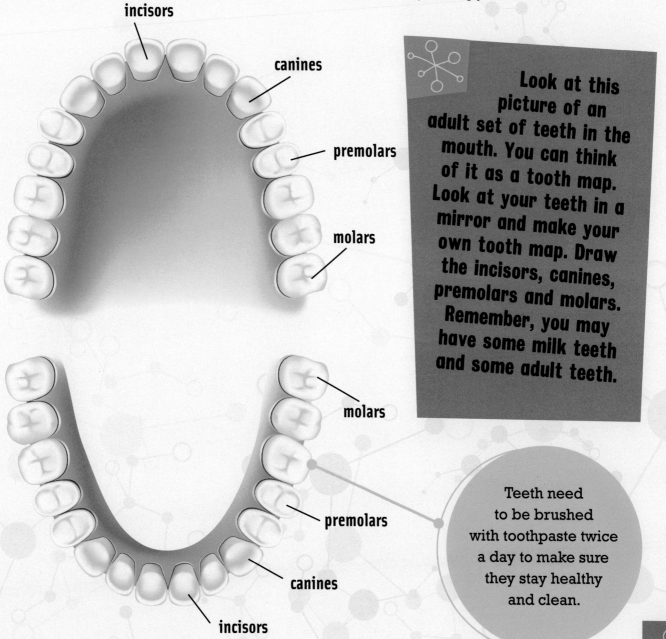

incisors

canines

premolars

molars

molars

premolars

canines

incisors

Look at this picture of an adult set of teeth in the mouth. You can think of it as a tooth map. Look at your teeth in a mirror and make your own tooth map. Draw the incisors, canines, premolars and molars. Remember, you may have some milk teeth and some adult teeth.

Teeth need to be brushed with toothpaste twice a day to make sure they stay healthy and clean.

The digestive system

Once your teeth have made food smaller, it goes on a journey through your digestive system. Food is digested so it can pass into the blood and go to the parts of the body that need it. The digestive system uses juices to break down the food, which the body uses for energy.

1 Mouth

2 Oesophagus

3 Stomach

Liver

Pancreas

4 Duodenum

6 Large intestine

5 Small intestine

7 Rectum and anus

1. Mouth

Your teeth break food into small pieces. Saliva is a **digestive juice** from your salivary **glands**, which makes your food slippery and even easier to swallow. Your tongue shapes your food into pellets, ready to pass down your oesophagus.

2. Oesophagus

The oesophagus or gullet is a tube in your throat. Food passes down the oesophagus from the back of your mouth to your stomach.

3. Stomach

The stomach churns up food and mixes it with digestive juices. Acid in the stomach helps to kill **germs** in food.

4. Duodenum

Bile from the liver and digestive juices from the pancreas are mixed with food here.

5. Small intestine

The small intestine makes more digestive juices to break down food further. The food then dissolves in the water that surrounds it. The wall of the small intestine **absorbs** all the **nutrients** and they pass into the blood. The dissolved nutrients in the blood are pumped round the body by the heart. Different body parts absorb them and use them to keep the body alive.

6. Large intestine

Undigested food passes through here and has water taken from it to be used by all parts of the body.

7. Rectum and anus

Undigested food is stored in the rectum. When the rectum is full, it is released out of the body through the anus.

The circulatory system

The digestive system breaks down food so that it can be passed to all parts of the body. The organs that carry digested food around the body are called the circulatory system.

The heart

Nearly all animals have a circulatory system powered by a heart. The heart pumps blood through the circulatory system. The circulatory system is made up of tubes which carry blood around the body.

An earthworm has tubes that act like hearts. Muscles in these tubes squeeze blood through the earthworm's circulatory system.

tubes

Your heart pumps blood around the body.
Your clenched fist is about the size of your heart.
To show you how fast your heart is beating, clench and unclench your fist twelve times in ten seconds.

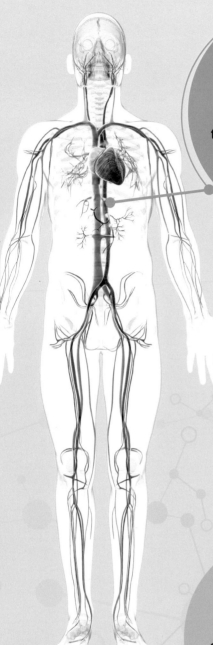

The blue tubes taking blood to the heart are called **veins**. The red tubes taking blood away from the heart are called **arteries**.

The human circulatory system

The heart in humans and vertebrates is divided into sections called chambers, which collect blood from one part of the circulatory system and push it into the next part. The human heart has four chambers. The two chambers on the right side collect blood from all round the body and send it to the lungs to get **oxygen**. The two on the left side collect blood containing oxygen from the lungs and send it all round the body. The oxygen is needed by all parts of the body to help change digested food into energy.

Cross-section of a heart

Each of the two upper chambers is called an atrium. The lower chambers are called ventricles.

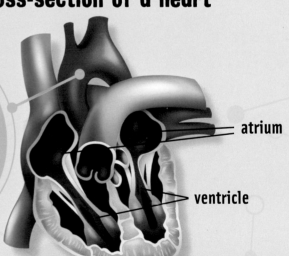

atrium

ventricle

Moving digested food

All the nutrients from digested food are absorbed into the blood from the small intestine. Veins take nutrient-filled blood to the heart. The heart then pumps this blood all over the body.

Nutrients

Bodies need nutrients, **fibre** and water to keep them alive. There are five groups of nutrients. These are **proteins**, **fats**, **carbohydrates**, **vitamins** and **minerals**. Food and drink provide us with nutrients and water.

Proteins

Proteins are needed for growth and to repair injuries to the body, such as cuts and bruises. They are also needed to make the juices that digest food.

Foods rich in proteins are meat, fish, beans, nuts and eggs.

Foods rich in carbohydrates include rice, pasta, bread and potatoes.

Carbohydrates

Carbohydrates contain energy. As soon as a carbohydrate-rich food has been digested, the body uses the energy to keep itself alive.

Vitamins

Vitamins help to keep the body healthy. For example, vitamin C is needed to keep blood vessels healthy and vitamin D is needed for healthy bones.

Fruit and vegetables are rich in vitamins.

Fats

The body stores fat under the skin to keep the body warm. Fat also contains energy. If the energy from carbohydrates has been used up and the body needs extra energy, it uses the energy in fats.

Butter and cheese are rich in fat.

Foods rich in minerals include milk, eggs and cereals.

Minerals

Minerals are used to build body parts, such as bones and blood.

A balanced diet

Your diet is the food that you usually eat every week. Your body needs a certain amount of each nutrient to keep it healthy. Too much or too little of a nutrient can make the body unhealthy.

A meal of pasta, meat, fresh vegetables and plenty of water will help to keep your body healthy.

A food pyramid

A **food pyramid** is a good guide to a balanced diet. Think of the food you eat during a week. If your diet is balanced you will be eating more foods from the bottom of the pyramid than from the top. A balanced diet would consist of lots of carbohydrates and fruit and vegetables, smaller amounts of protein and very little fat or sugar.

If you eat too many foods at the top of a food pyramid, you may have an unhealthy diet.

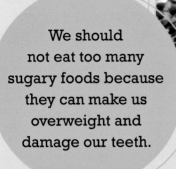

We should not eat too many sugary foods because they can make us overweight and damage our teeth.

Sugar and fatty foods

Sugar and fat supply the body with energy. The energy in sugar and fat can be used straight away. If too much sugar and fat is eaten, the body stores it as fat under the skin. Too much sugar and fat in our diet can cause **obesity**. This condition can affect the health of the body in many ways, such as causing heart disease or damaging bones and joints because the body becomes too heavy for the skeleton to support it.

Snacking on crisps and other fatty foods can make you put on weight.

?

At the end of the day, write down everything you have eaten. Did you eat a balanced diet? Use the food pyramid to help you.

What animals eat

Animals can be divided into three groups according to what they eat: **herbivores, carnivores** and **omnivores**.

Herbivores

Herbivores feed only on plants. Slugs and snails feed on leaves and are examples of invertebrate herbivores. Vertebrate herbivores include some birds, which feed on seeds; and some mammals, such as sheep and deer, which feed on grass.

Tortoises eat the leaves of plants. They are vertebrate herbivores.

The caterpillars of moths and butterflies feed on leaves. They are invertebrate herbivores.

Carnivores

Carnivores feed only on other animals. Invertebrate carnivores include spiders, which eat insects; and centipedes, which eat insects and spiders. Sharks, which eat fish, dolphins and seals; and frogs, which eat insects, are both examples of vertebrate carnivores.

Lions eat zebras and antelope. They are vertebrate carnivores.

Pigs eat vegetables, fruit and insects. They are vertebrate omnivores.

Omnivores

Omnivores feed on both plants and animals. Humans are omnivores. A crab is an example of an invertebrate omnivore. It eats worms, prawns and seaweed. Bears eat berries and fish; squirrels eat nuts and birds' eggs. They are both examples of vertebrate omnivores.

Are pets herbivores, carnivores or omnivores? What do your pets eat? What do your friends' pets eat? Using books and the internet, check to see whether your pets are receiving the correct diet.

Food chains

We have seen that animals can be put into groups according to what they eat. Scientists have studied what animals eat in their **habitats** and have linked the animals by the food that they eat. The links are joined together to make a **food chain**. A food chain shows how food passes from one living thing to another in a habitat.

Links in a food chain

plant   herbivore   omnivore

A plant takes in the sunlight that falls on its leaves, carbon dioxide from the air, and water and minerals from the soil. It uses them to make nutrients. A plant is the first link in a food chain. When herbivores and omnivores feed on a plant they take in its nutrients, becoming the second link in the food chain. The third link is a carnivore or omnivore, which eats the herbivore or plant-eating omnivore, completing the food chain.

Grass is the first link in the food chain. A rabbit is eating the grass. It is the second link in the food chain.

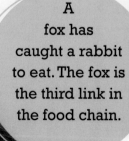

A fox has caught a rabbit to eat. The fox is the third link in the food chain.

Prey and predators

Animals that are eaten by other animals are called **prey**. Animals that eat other animals are called **predators**. In the three-link food chain on page 26 the rabbit is the prey and the fox is the predator. A food chain can have more than three links, like this one.

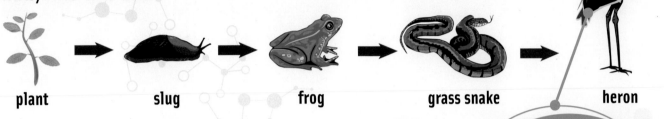

plant → slug → frog → grass snake → heron

Humans in food chains

Humans are in food chains too. When a human eats a plant they are the second link in the food chain.

apple → human

This food chain has five links. The plant is eaten by the slug. The slug is prey to the frog. The frog is prey to the grass snake. The grass snake is prey to the heron.

If a human eats meat, they become the third link in the food chain.

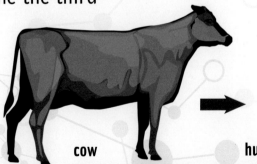

grass → cow → human

Work out more food chains with humans in them.
Are humans herbivores, carnivores or omnivores?
Can you think of a four-link food chain with a human as the third link?

Glossary

Absorb to take in. A sponge absorbs water. The small intestine absorbs nutrients.

Amphibians an animal that spends its early life as a tadpole in water and its later life as a land animal, such as a frog or toad.

Arteries tubes in the circulatory system that take blood away from the heart.

Bile a liquid that breaks up fats to aid digestion.

Brain the part of the body that controls all of the body's activities.

Carbohydrates a group of foods that provide the body with energy.

Carnivore an animal that eats other animals.

Cartilage the slippery covering of bones in a joint.

Contract to get shorter or smaller.

Digestive juice a liquid that breaks down food into small pieces so it can dissolve in the water in the digestive system.

Exoskeleton a hard covering used to support and protect some invertebrates.

Fats a group of foods that provide the body with energy. Fat also creates a layer beneath the skin which helps keep the body warm.

Fibre a material found in cereals and bread that is not digested, but instead helps food move along the digestive system.

Food chain a group of living things linked together to show how they are related to each other by feeding. Food chains show how food moves from one living thing to another.

Food pyramid a diagram used to show the quantities of different foods we should eat to stay healthy.

Germs very tiny living things that cause diseases and make the body ill.

Gland part of the body that makes chemicals for use in the body. The salivary glands for example make a juice called saliva. Saliva covers food as it is chewed to help digestion.

Habitat the home of a living thing.

Herbivore an animal that eats plants.

Ligament a cord which joins the bones together in a joint.

Mammals vertebrate animals with fur or feathers, such as mice, humans and bears. Most give birth to live babies that feed on milk from their mother.

Minerals a group of nutrients that are needed to build body parts.

MRI scanner a machine that uses a magnetic force to take pictures of what is inside the body.

Nerves parts of the body that carry messages from the sense organs to the brain and messages from the brain to other parts of the body.

Nutrients materials that are needed by the body for growth, injury repair, health and all activities in the body that keep it alive.

Obesity the condition of being overweight.

Omnivore an animal that eats both plants and animals.

Oxygen a gas used by animals to release energy from digested food.

Predator an animal that feeds on other animals.

Prey an animal that is eaten by other animals.

Proteins a group of foods that provide materials to help the body grow and repair its injuries.

Reptiles animals such as crocodiles that have scaly skin and lay eggs on land.

Segments a section or part of something.

Senses the body's five ways of finding out about the world around it. Sight, smell, hearing, taste and touch are our five senses.

Spinal cord a long white bundle of nerves that runs down the back inside the backbone.

Tendon a cord that attaches a muscle to a bone.

Thorax the chest of a vertebrate animal and the middle part of the body of an insect.

Torso the part of the body to which the head, arms and legs are attached.

Veins tubes in the circulatory system that take blood away from the heart.

Vertebra one of the bones that makes up the backbone.

Vitamins nutrients found in foods such as fruit and vegetables. Vitamins help to keep the body healthy.

X-rays invisible rays that can pass through the body. They can be used to make a photograph to show the position of bones.

Answers to the activities and questions

Page 15 Teeth

Activity: The map will depend on how many teeth you have lost from your first set. Leave a gap in the map where a tooth is missing. You may like to make a map again, perhaps in a few months, and record any changes.

Page 18 The circulatory system

Activity: You have to work quickly to clench and unclench your fist twelve times in ten seconds. Imagine how hard your heart is working every second of every day!

Page 9 Muscles

Answer: Your biceps get softer and increase in length when your arm is straightened. Your triceps get harder and decrease in length when your arm is straightened.

Page 11 Animal skeletons

Activity: The water-filled balloon will support weight, such as this book. Be careful, a very heavy weight will pop the balloon and send water everywhere!

Page 23 A balanced diet

Activity: Make a list of the foods you have for breakfast, lunch and dinner. Compare the foods with the ones in the pyramid and see if you are eating more of the foods at the bottom than at the top.

If you eat more foods from the bottom of the pyramid and fewer from the top, your diet has a good balance of nutrients.

Page 25 What animals eat

Activity: Make a list of the foods you feed to each pet over a week. You may like to construct a table grouping the pets into herbivores, carnivores and omnivores based on your results. There are many books on pet care and websites, such as the RSPCA, which provide advice on feeding pets to keep them healthy.

Page 27 Food chains

Activity: Examples include:

corn (grain) → chicken → human

carrot → human

potato → human

grass → lamb → human.

Humans are omnivores.

Think of yourself as a prey animal and think of an animal that might eat people! The food chain could be:

grass → lamb → human → alligator.

Index

About this book

Moving Up with Science is designed to help children develop the following skills:

Science enquiry skills: researching using secondary sources, all pages but specifically the activity on page 27; grouping and classifying, page 15; observing over time, pages 9, 23; comparative or fair testing, pages 7, 11; pattern seeking, pages 9, 19.

Working scientifically skills: making careful observations, pages 7, 9, 11, 15; setting up simple practical enquiries, pages 7, 11; making a comparative or fair test, page 7; using results to draw simple conclusions, pages 7, 9, 11; using straightforward scientific evidence to answer questions, pages 15, 23, 25, 27.

Critical thinking skills: knowledge, all pages; comprehension, page 27; analysis, pages 23, 25.